P9-EMM-910

We Need Principals

by Jane Scoggins Bauld

Consulting Editor: Gail Saunders-Smith, Ph.D.

Consultant: E. Joseph Schneider
Deputy Executive Director
American Association of School Administrators

Pebble Books

an imprint of Capstone Press
Mankato, Minnesota

SOUTH HUNTINGTON
PUBLIC LIBRARY
2 MELVILLE ROAD
HUNTINGTON STATION, N.Y. 11746

Pebble Books are published by Capstone Press
151 Good Counsel Drive, P.O. Box 669, Mankato, Minnesota 56002
http://www.capstone-press.com

Copyright © 2000 Capstone Press. All rights reserved.
No part of this book may be reproduced without written permission
from the publisher. The publisher takes no responsibility for the use of any
of the materials or methods described in this book, nor for the products thereof.
Printed in the United States of America.

1 2 3 4 5 6 05 04 03 02 01 00

Library of Congress Cataloging-in-Publication Data
Bauld, Jane Scoggins.
    We need principals/by Jane Scoggins Bauld.
    p. cm.—(Helpers in our school)
    Includes bibliographical references and index.
    Summary: Simple text and photographs present principals and their role in
elementary schools.
    ISBN 0-7368-0532-X
    1. School principals—Juvenile literature. [1. School principals. 2. Occupations.]
I. Title. II. Series.
LB2831.9 .B38   2000
371.2′012—dc21   99-046801

Note to Parents and Teachers

The Helpers in Our School series supports national social studies
standards for how groups and institutions work to meet individual
needs. This book describes principals and illustrates what they do
in schools. The photographs support early readers in understanding
the text. The repetition of words and phrases helps early readers
learn new words. This book also introduces early readers to subject-
specific vocabulary words, which are defined in the Words to Know
section. Early readers may need assistance to read some words and
to use the Table of Contents, Words to Know, Read More, Internet
Sites, and Index/Word List sections of the book.

Table of Contents

A principal is the leader of a school.

A principal hires teachers.

A principal helps teachers plan what to teach.

10

A principal visits classrooms.

A principal talks
with students.

A principal talks
with parents.

A principal tells
the community about
the school.

A principal makes rules.

The principal's rules help keep students safe.

Words to Know

classroom—a room in a school where classes take place; principals visit classrooms to watch how teachers and students work together.

community—a group of people who live in the same area

hire—to pay someone to do a job; principals hire teachers to teach students.

plan—to decide how something will be done; principals and teachers work together to plan what students will learn.

principal—a person who leads a school; principals help plan what students will learn and make decisions about school business.

student—a person who goes to a school to learn; principals talk with students about learning.

teacher—a person who helps others learn and solve problems; teachers and principals work together to plan what teachers will teach.

Read More

Boraas, Tracey. *School Principals.* Community Helpers. Mankato, Minn.: Bridgestone Books, 1999.

Greene, Carol. *At the School.* Chanhassen, Minn.: Child's World, 1998.

Internet Sites

Education Administrators
http://stats.bls.gov/oco/ocos007.htm

National Association of Elementary School Principals
http://www.naesp.org

Welcome to EduNET
http://www.edunetconnect.com

Index/Word List

Word Count: 53
Early-Intervention Level: 6

Editorial Credits
Martha E. H. Rustad, editor; Abby Bradford, Bradfordesign, Inc., cover designer; Kia Bielke, production designer; Kimberly Danger, photo researcher

Photo Credits
Kim Stanton, 6
Marilyn Moseley LaMantia, 12, 16, 18
Matt Swinden, 10
Michael Krasowitz/FPG International LLC, 4
Photri-Microstock/Spencer Grant, cover
Shaffer Photography/James L. Shaffer, 1, 8, 14
Visuals Unlimited/Nancy Alexander, 20

24